(NEVERTHELESS ENJOYMENT

(NEVERTHELESS ENJOYMENT

Elizabeth Bryant

Quale Press

Portions of this book were published in *Coconut, Dusie, Gerry Mulligan* and *Wheelhouse Magazine.*

The author wishes to thank Andrew Gray, Jennie Neighbors, Alex Kahn, Celia Bland, Robert Kelly, and Lily Ruth Bryant for their support and guidance.

Cover design and artwork by Alex Kahn. The wood-grain image is courtesy of Monarch Interiors. The Hurricane Juan photo is courtesy of Jacques Descloitres, MODIS Land Rapid Response Team at NASA GSFC.

ISBN: 978-0-9792999-9-5 trade paperback edition

LCCN: 2009938617

Quale Press
www.quale.com

For Anna McLellan
who knows sometimes there is not a word for it,
and so it goes untranslated.

At this stage, a concise definition of Lacan's notion of *jouissance*[*] is necessary. *Jouissance* is definitely not pleasure: on the contrary, it is precisely that which "goes beyond" Freud's pleasure principle. The main characteristic of *jouissance* is suffering: however, we are dealing here with a kind of suffering which is not simply unpleasant, and consequently cannot merely be related to pleasure in an oppositional way.

—Lorenzo Chiesa, *Lacan: The Silent Partners*

[*]The word, or the idea of, *jouissance* resists simple translation. In English, *enjoyment* is often offered for consideration.

of the word)

Slumps in the middle where history is. That weight long ago. An initial utterance, whereas it may be forgivable, remains irretrievable. You were placed, then, by the fall of its shadow. A blanket already thick with the years ahead. Or beside you, a penumbral mist. This is a life, I can tell you. However coated it may already be before you emerge within it.

of what the word was, where history is)

Spoken again, coming toward you. First as single sound, then later as an index. Pictured, presently, and because of lack of an actual example, as a grocery list. Things you need. Things you need to get. That you've had before. That get used up. And requests made by others, for other things. That you've never had. You can't say what for.

in what, as in what it is to say)

When a repeated phrase seems without thought, and no longer meant.
That its employment is effortless in the worst sense.

of the weather)

Slips across always left to right as in a sentence. We read the same way, or were taught to. If words come through as errors, then. Or if words come through.

and its suggestion)

Recesses of the grove where the core is primed to receive them. Warblers, flycatchers, and finches in migration.

A streamlined body and lightweight skeleton minimize resistance.

wanting something)

From up against it. Stepping alongside a number of others.

when held by the embankment)

I kept thinking aubergine, but it wasn't. The color of the water was no color that night. Only presence and absence of light, in peaks and eddies. Seeing things. You, for instance. Perched with feet dangling above. The river folding over itself in full muscle. Insects heard but invisible.

and disremembered words)

These lie in chains just beneath your skin. Consult them as if running your finger through the grime layered plasti-glass covering a subway map. They are as unknown to you as the connections at Carroll Gardens.

in emergence and the discomfort it causes)

Varieties of iris have staggered bloom times. Reticulata being among the earliest, Japanese the latest. Each blooms once. An undisclosed repudiation of nonce.

in the back of his head)

Where's the door? It's mostly unlocked. Mostly unlocked places he goes to. Lingers only where doors are seldom locked.

in a forkful of mussel)

Fed across the table. Speared then carried—an idea—to my mouth.
Someone else would let the sauce drip, or push the whole plate instead.
Behind your gesture is a humid landscape punctured by verdigris spires
and cars going all to hell. There are women older than their mothers
were when first babies were born, and men content at last with second
wives. Behind your gesture is a small town. Its inhabitants arrive in the
telltale raiments of a posse, and they love to tell you what to do. How
to prepare an egg. Where to put your stubborn appetite for affection.

seeing something)

As if you could see anything from here. See, see you. Seeing you with eyes seeing not. They're not seeing. They don't have eyes in the backs of their heads, a gift given only to mothers. Eyes at the back of my head. I see seeing. See you, and nothing. At least I know it's nothing.

estimating future events)

In late July cool weather is unexpected for many days at a time, and should not contain winds belonging to early November. Today I want you to be less correct than you are. Have it turn out that you forgot to measure twice.

knowing how)

Some secretive shy birds must be flushed out. Flying away, you catch a glimpse. You get a clear shot. Some species of birds you see only when they are dead.

of you, as a selection of sentences)

Some of us become of the words their lovers.

Because if it were said some other way, you would simply take it for a sentence you've seen or heard before, then stop listening. Quickly, then, distinguish between the list of words for speaking, and ones consigned to a sarcophagus. That is, eater of flesh. Its meaning slides across time.

on a mattress)

To make note of any one thing. The way you come, for example. Then
there is a difference. I know there was at least a before, even as you
refuse some meanwhile. I mean while you spilled warm across my back,
I took note: that is unlike—or you are not—him.

alongside a long-term strategy)

Appear close to flight at all times.

in the night beside)

Being pulled in. And toward. And with hands on. Your hands on. You pull with your eyes closed. You pull blind. Me to. Me to it. Me to you and. And the fear of it. And fear being something. Desirable. Something. Expressible. If I express. Awake in the night. Light sleepers, we two. Listen. I'm a feather beside you. Over you. Turning over and over in the air as you breathe. Sleep light.

over a joint smoked on I-87 north of Saratoga)

Red has an imaginary function. I write to tell a friend I've only just realized that to have some sort of faith in yourself can be psychotic in the right light. Or wrong. Stop stop stop and go. Stop stop stop and go. My favorite color is to stop. I believe a bull sees this and he goes. These are things we know about these things. These are things we are told. I don't make this stuff up. I have said entirely too much.

aiding your every desire so that I may become it)

My hands cupped around your hands cupped around your match
fighting off a March wind damp on rue Sainte-Catherine to light your
cigarette. We're lost. I don't smoke.

making a list of what you wanted but didn't end up getting in French)

chaussures de montagne, chandail, chapeau, cahier, mètre ruban

in an envelope)

His is bubble shaped but not round. She sees this or he thinks it.
Imperfect origin. She thinks she sees this, so that he knows she does, or
worries about it. Not quite round, or even strenuously irregular.

of a body)

Is not what we're after. Sneak up to it wearing a slip and then sense. Disagreement between bare knees, and whether it's the silk itself or its habit of following a curve precisely. Not the curve, but when the selection moved toward you. Your word for it.

in the sharp cold sparkling night sky, rapid drop in temperature—
another one)

Watch his hands when he speaks, thinks, drinks wine, eats dinner,
touches anything. Stand with legs and teeth chattering while he explains.
What is wanted. Hands across elm boards, pointing to marks of strange
beauty. A certain kind of wood-rot—like the noble rot of some grapes
enables the production of Tokaji or Sauternes—causes discolored ring
patterns. A desirable error of nature. Lovely and something to preserve.
Careful not to cut that part out. Spalting.

alongside unprocessed longing)

I never bothered to lock it when he spent the night. His front door also sometimes was locked. I tried once, twice maybe from the street. I fell asleep on the curb there almost, drunk one night he wasn't there.

of resistance)

He intends not to be taken altogether.

of a stray black hair)

Left behind and stuck to the yellow flannel sheet. Curled and small and mildly wiry, it might hail from anywhere: back, nose, leg, ass, toe. I pin it to a page with clear tape and mark the date.

in an image of you rising from the smoke of a burning mosquito coil)

This whole portion of your cheek not shadowed. I found its expanse difficult to render in convincing bounding lines. Something kept appearing then claimed to be missing. I walked across that section. Its white a shade of faded blood orange when placed, side by side, on the same deflated down pillow as my own cheek, tepid and the color of a garbanzo bean. That part I left alone. Not a blur, but a lie. Because I did not know what to put there, I put nothing. I walked across that section. Paced as if my steps could better guess content.

of a head smacked in afterthought)

What I meant to say. In ordinary language. To the point as if lifted straight from our friend the dictionary. A thing of speaking. A collection of all there is to say.

in a barkeep saying no)

Don't know. Haven't seen him. Not tonight. Rained, so water falls out of my hair onto the dark oak and between empty glasses. He rubs a drop away with the pointer-man of his right hand and tells me a soft *sorry.*

when days pass)

You come across to me in pieces as ever. In the gaps are songs of waking frogs and sudden snaps as wood acclimates. I receive and receive but never capture. Fragments accumulate the same as many thousands-thick monarch butterflies arriving. Not a blanket, only appearing to be one at an uninformed glance.

in an advancing storm)

And all its persuasiveness comes across. See it coming. The way a mother sees a shoe as an accident on the stairs. Her extra eyes opened at expulsion of the afterbirth.

being the sort of person who says)

You were thinking in response to while we're fucking.

and review)

Say it over and over to the darkness of the bedroom at 2 a.m. after waking from another dream in which his indifference is so presupposed it might as well be air for breathing. Air in the dream. When I wake, it's difficult to breathe at first. Almost nothing has happened—he tolerates my presence but doesn't engage or acknowledge, and this appears to concern him not at all. And yet I wake to, or because of, a crushing inability to mitigate, to effect. Nothing I do does anything at all. Nothing has happened, yet I can't breathe.

of what, in what was wanted)

Little dark flower cup a black mouth or slippershaped flower. You don't make me want to figure out the perfect way of speaking about you. I try but nothing more comes outside of what's obvious about you, which is that you find yourself lingeringly attached to a stalk by a tension unseen but slightly understood by non-flowers. I speak for myself when I say I am surprised each time petals all drop off at once rather than remain attached to slowly wither.

and desire)

Another word for that. Find one. To find one. To find it first then compare. The problem with being alone. The problem of being faced with your own other word for it. The problem of being faced with your own other word for a lack of it. Some girls want what other girls want. Some girls want what boys want. If you're alone what is your word for it? If you're alone is your word for it still a word? When you have a word for it is it the word? Is it the word someone else has? Some girls have a word. Some girls have the same word boys have. Some words make the same word as the word for it, some want to. As if it could want to. As if a word could.

in an archive)

A collection of all you are capable of saying.

and deposits)

However infrequent, accumulate nonetheless. An assemblage of sprockets joists carabiners and kick-wax molds a serviceable likeness. It's possible to proceed this way, indefinitely informed by parted-out miscreations.

or an explanation)

Taken in a stream, particles and objects deposited all along, all along, may be rubricized. He recalls each one, then displays a helpless amnesia, so it might as well be forgotten. But before the privacy of sleep and while soaping his boy parts in the shower (after work, in the morning), he knows. Shoves it from the nest, but imperfectly.

.

of the tracks)

Let's look at worn. Let's look at distortion. Let's look at sizes, at numbers, at repeating. Let's look at direction, at direction, which direction. Let's look at beside them. Let's look at sliding off to the side, the slurring of edges. Let's look at what it is, what it was. Let's look at residue. Particulates. Intentions. What was meant. What you meant to do. Let's look at going. Let's look at talking. Articulates. Inertia. Let's look at facts. Let's look at looking. At together. Look together. Keep looking. Let's look at it. Reminders. Remainders. Let's look at looking, and a tolerance. To have one. Let's look at seeing. What particulars. What they are. Then say them.

declaring she is gypsy, or not)

Leave you two. Leave you to it. Her flamenco air (flutter black dress, high black shoes). Her hair of urgency, pulled back. Pulled black. Her black eye skip. Her sentence skip. Over me to you. You too. I see you too. Leave you to it. To the dress with a zip, its air of scarcely there. Its press into skin. Its impress on you. Leave it to you.

in this phenomenological residual image)

A version of me, coming in pictures, sentences, and projected sounds.
Like Os and uh-ohs.

in the morning, and the sweat broke around 3:30)

Now become one of those who slip away without saying. Find a sock and an earring. In the dim light, the red shadowed brown bare light of pre-dawn. Through the parts already there. There are a few things already there. Over there. A laundry pile. Over there a book. Open, face down. Now become one of those. Find boots and a sweater. Who slip them on without waking. You sleeping. Slip them on in the dim, in the color of a flower part. A sepal. Red sepal. Papers and photos. Find my things and put them on. Find things. The unfamiliar scrawl of a handwritten note. The wherewithal to slip away in a dim light.

exists through enumeration of hated things)

Christian names. Baby greens. Artisan vinegars. Serialized emotions. Waiting.

without capture)

Can't be done. As effective in achieving its goal as a sleeveless gown is worn by an armless woman.

in the rearview)

Again sounds like *not enough.*

in what, as in what I learn from you)

How not to have a feeling. Go fish-eyed all over. The whole body a chilly membrane shot through with parts we don't eat. The meat that would be the eye of a fish. Always cold when whole, then dissolved into the texture of a shriveled contact lens after cooking.

at the drop-leaf kitchen table, visited by disproportionate cogencies)

The experience of bone. Its bogus claims of interiority and support.

in an *other* word for it, namely, pomegranate)

She isn't rose-breasted at all but deeply striped, white and brown, nearly big as a robin. And she isn't her name, with birders in pursuit of the unequivocal male.

of an inability to cast a shadow)

An appearance of calling me beside the point. Thought of as such. No reflection on you.

in un-shot footage)

A sequence in which a bad outcome is subsequently revealed as apocryphal. Over a short period of time. We are seen quickly, eventually, tethering distances between us.

in the end)

Again it ends, again. I say I hate repetition but I mean routine. Not so much that shit happens, but repetition, and no knowledge increase.

on an unfinished table top)

When life stops. No more trips outside. The ones you can't avoid. It's playful until it becomes the thing you meant not to do. Having eaten too much or waited too long. Now too full. Now forced to keep still.

in the worst sense)

Bone is not the hollow super-structure of bird skeleton, mechanized for flight. Filled with derivatives strengthened on impact and use, it will get you like the word. With sudden breaks and apprehension.

around a Chinese apple)

Eaten. Not as an apple, as I have come to understand apple. But as a poem is realized. Not as appearance, but evidence. Scholarship, in the sense that I know a female rose-breasted grosbeak—her bill, pale and larger than average for the size of her body; a question of proportions—when I see one, and this by way of kitchen windows, and time given to few visitors. The drab-colored female being more of a challenge.

quale [kwa-lay]: *Eng* n 1. A property (such as hardness) considered apart from things that have that property. 2. A property that is experienced as distinct from any source it may have in a physical object. *Ital.* pron.a. 1. Which, what. 2. Who. 3. Some. 4. As, just as.

※

Made in the USA
Monee, IL
07 July 2026